W9-AUK-776

A Taste of Culture

FOODS OF ITALY

Barbara Sheen

KIDHAVEN PRESS

An imprint of Thomson Gale, a part of The Thomson Corporation

THOMSON

™

GALE

Detroit • New York • San Francisco • San Diego • New Haven, Conn. • Waterville, Maine • London • Munich

© 2006 by KidHaven Press. KidHaven Press is an imprint of The Gale Group, Inc., a division of Thomson Learning, Inc.

KidHaven™ and Thomson Learning™ are trademarks used herein under license.

For more information, contact
KidHaven Press
27500 Drake Rd.
Farmington Hills, MI 48331-3535
Or you can visit our Internet site at http://www.gale.com

LIBRARY OF CONGRESS CATALOGING-IN-PUBLICATION DATA

Sheen, Barbara.
  Foods of Italy / by Barbara Sheen.
    p. cm. — (A taste of culture)
  Includes bibliographical references and index.
  ISBN 0-7377-3034-X (hard cover : alk. paper)
  1. Cookery, Italian—Juvenile literature. 2. Italy—Social life and customs—Juvenile literature. I. Title. II. Series.
  TX723.S43 2005
  394.1'20945—dc22

                                           2004026721

Printed in the United States of America

Contents

The Heart and Soul of Italian Cooking

Say the word Italy, and the first thing that comes to many peoples' minds is food! Fresh ingredients, savory spices, creamy cheeses, and golden oils make Italian cooking famous throughout the world. Four essential ingredients give Italian food its unique flavor. These ingredients—tomatoes, olive oil, garlic, and Parmesan cheese—are the heart and soul of Italian cooking.

Olive Oil: An Essential Ingredient

Italians use olive oil in almost everything. Olive oil is the first ingredient an Italian cook puts in a pan. Tomatoes, garlic, and onions are browned in it. Eggs are fried in it. Vegetables are sprinkled with it. Fish is preserved in it. Meat is rubbed with it, then grilled or broiled.

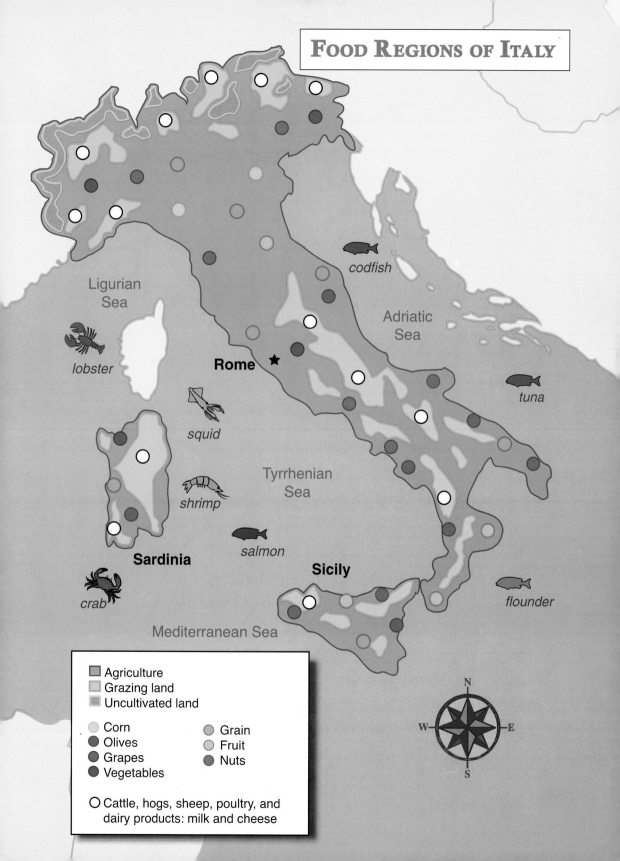

FOOD REGIONS OF ITALY

Ligurian
Sea

codfish

lobster

Rome

Adriatic
Sea

tuna

squid

Tyrrhenian
Sea

shrimp

Sardinia

salmon

Sicily

crab

flounder

Mediterranean Sea

Agriculture
Grazing land
Uncultivated land

Corn   Grain
Olives   Fruit
Grapes   Nuts
Vegetables

○ Cattle, hogs, sheep, poultry, and
  dairy products: milk and cheese

N
W — E
S

A group of Italians enjoys a snack of fresh bread dipped in extra-virgin olive oil and topped with tomatoes and onions.

An Italian salad is considered bare unless it is dressed with olive oil, minced garlic, and vinegar. Olive oil mixed with garlic bathes pasta in a golden sauce. Little bowls of olive oil spiced with basil and oregano grace every Italian table, and diners dip crusty bread in the mixture.

Making olive oil involves placing olives into a metal-toothed grinder that squeezes or presses the oil out of them. Olives are put through the grinder many times. After each pressing, oil is extracted. Oil that has been pressed many times is used for cooking and frying. Extra-virgin olive oil, which is taken from the first pressing, is the finest olive oil. It is golden and fragrant. Italians use it on salads, breads, and **pasta**. Mario Batali, an Italian cooking expert, explains that he "pours the freshly pressed nectar on everything we eat, from toast at breakfast to raw vegetables . . . at dinner."[1]

An Ancient Delight

Italians have been producing and using olive oil since ancient times. Archaeologists say olive trees have been growing in Italy for 20 million years, and Italian cooks have been using the oil since the 5th century B.C. The ancient Romans treasured olive oil. They believed it gave people strength and long life. Interestingly, modern scientists agree. They say that a diet rich in olive oil helps protect people from heart disease and diabetes.

Italians have been producing olive oil since ancient times. Here, a farmer sorts through a bin of olives before they are pressed into oil.

This may be why Italians do not get these diseases as frequently as other people.

Olive oil is so important to Italians that there is an olive oil museum in Venice. At the museum, visitors can taste dozens of different kinds of olive oil and view ancient artifacts that teach them about the oil's history.

Tomatoes: Dangerous Fruits

Tomatoes are as much a part of Italian cooking as olive oil. It is hard to imagine Italian cooking without these plump, juicy fruits. But tomatoes were not always popular in Italy. Historians say that explorer Christopher Columbus brought the first tomatoes to Italy in 1522. These were small yellow tomatoes, which the Italians named pomis d'oro, or "golden apples." Many Italians believed these first tomatoes were poisonous. Eventually, a brave, or hungry, Italian ate one. When nothing happened, other daring Italians followed suit. The early Italians found that adding bits of tomato to a plate of pasta or a pot of beans gave these bland dishes a sweet, rich taste. It didn't take long for Italians to fall in love with tomatoes.

Over time, Italians' passion for tomatoes grew. Today the bright red fruits grow all over Italy—in farms in central and southern Italy; at the base of Italy's volcanoes, Mt. Etna and Mt. Vesuvius; in backyard gardens; and in clay pots on city dwellers' balconies. Italians grow hundreds of different types of tomatoes—fat, red beefsteaks, plum-shaped romas, bite-sized cherry tomatoes, purple grape tomatoes, pear-shaped yellow tomatoes—each with their

Spaghetti with Garlic and Oil

Spaghetti with garlic and oil is a favorite Italian dish that uses two important ingredients: garlic and olive oil. Linguine or other long pastas can be used instead of spaghetti, and a fresh-sliced tomato and Parmesan cheese can be tossed into the spaghetti before serving.

Ingredients:

1/3 cup olive oil
2 to 3 cloves of chopped garlic
12 ounces spaghetti
salt and pepper to taste

Instructions:

1. Prepare the spaghetti according to the package directions.
2. While the spaghetti is cooking, heat a pan over low heat.
3. When the pan is warm, add the olive oil.
4. Once the oil is warm, add the garlic, stirring often. Add salt and pepper to taste. The garlic is done when it is golden. Do not let the garlic get brown or it will taste bitter.
5. Drain the spaghetti and put it into a large serving bowl.
6. Add the cooked, drained spaghetti to the garlic and oil.
7. Toss thoroughly to coat the spaghetti. Serve hot.

Serves 4

Harvesting Olives

To make olive oil, first, Italians must harvest the olives. To harvest olives, farmers place large pieces of cloth under the trees. Then they beat the trees with long sticks. This causes the olives to fall onto the cloths. Having the cloths under the trees to catch the olives makes it easy for the farmers to harvest the olives without having to scramble on the ground gathering one olive at a time.

own distinctive flavor. As one Italian farmer says, "You say tomatoes—you think Italy."[2]

The Essential Ingredient in Sauces

Italians harvest tomatoes in late summer, when they are ripe and at the height of their freshness. Fresh raw tomatoes are sliced, drizzled with olive oil, and layered between thin pieces of mozzarella cheese. They are tossed with pasta, used to top **pizza**, and mashed on toast with bits of garlic.

Most importantly, tomatoes are slowly cooked with herbs, garlic, oil, and a pinch of sugar to make lots of different, rich, pungent sauces that top pastas, meats, fish, and vegetables. Italian sauces are famous throughout the world, and most Italian sauces contain tomatoes.

Workers unload crates of tomatoes along a canal in Venice. Tomatoes are the main ingredient in many Italian sauces.

To bring the fresh taste of summer to Italian dishes all year long, Italians can and sun dry ripe tomatoes. Rows of canned tomatoes are a common sight in Italian homes.

Garlic

Italians love herbs and spices. They use them to add zest to their cooking. Garlic is the most popular. Italians use garlic to bring out the flavor in food in the same way that Americans use salt and pepper. Almost every Italian sauce contains a few cloves of minced garlic. Garlic is routinely rubbed on toasted bread. Italians season meat, poultry, fish, seafood, beans, and vegetables with garlic.

Italians roast whole garlic bulbs in their ovens. The delicious scent fills Italian kitchens. Both the scent of garlic and the sight of it are common in Italian homes. **Garlic braids** decorate many Italian kitchens. Garlic braids are made of garlic bulbs that are woven together to form long strands. They provide an appealing and practical way to store garlic. Italian cooks pluck garlic bulbs off the braid whenever they need them.

Like olive oil, the ancient Romans used garlic. Roman soldiers were given garlic everyday. The Romans thought it would make the soldiers stronger and braver. Modern Italians prefer garlic for its good taste. It is hard to find an Italian dish that doesn't contain the savory spice. Italian chef Marcella Hazan explains: "If there were no longer any garlic, the **cuisine**

A woman at an outdoor market in Rome drapes an enormous garlic braid over her shoulder as she shops for fresh produce.

would be hard to recognize. What would roast chicken be like without garlic, or . . . pasta sauces?"[3]

Parmesan Cheese

Italy is also well known for its cheeses. In fact, hundreds of different cheeses are made in Italy. But Parmesan cheese is far and away the most common and most essential cheese used in Italian cooking.

Tomato Bruschetta

Bruschetta is the Italian word for toast. But instead of using a toaster, bruschetta is toasted over a fire or in a broiler. Bruschetta is usually served as an appetizer before a meal, and it is eaten with a knife and fork. This recipe uses ripe tomatoes—cherry, grape, or roma tomatoes are best.

Ingredients:

4 slices Italian bread
2 cloves of garlic, peeled and chopped
$1/2$ cup extra-virgin olive oil
2 cups chopped tomatoes
2 tablespoons olive oil
3 tablespoons fresh, chopped basil
salt and pepper to taste

Instructions:

1. Mix together the tomatoes with the olive oil, basil, salt, and pepper.
2. Place the bread in a broiler or on a grill. Cook the bread until it is golden.
3. Turn the bread over and repeat.
4. Remove the bread from the heat.
5. Put a fourth of the tomato mixture on each slice of bread, and serve.

Serves 4

Colorful wheels of cheese and long strands of sausage are offered for sale at an outdoor market in southern Italy.

Parmesan cheese has a mellow, salty flavor. The best Parmesan cheese comes from Parma and Reggio-Emilia, two neighboring regions of north-central Italy where cows graze on special grasses that are believed to give the cheese its rich flavor. The cheese that is made from their milk is formed into giant wheels, which weigh about 60 pounds (27kg) each. The wheels are aged for two to three years before they are sent to stores. This makes Parmesan cheese quite expensive. Italians pay ten to twelve dollars a pound for the cheese, but they agree that it is worth it.

A Little Goes a Long Way

Italians buy chunks of the cheese, which they grate themselves and sprinkle on pasta, rice, bread, salads, vegetables, soups, and stews. Just a little bit goes a long

The Cheeses of Italy

Parmesan cheese is just one of the many cheeses that Italians love. Mozarella cheese is another important Italian cheese. White and mild tasting, mozzarella cheese is sold in large balls that weigh about 1 pound (.45kg) each. It is used to top pizza and pasta dishes.

Gorgonzola cheese, a blue-veined cheese, is another Italian favorite. It is dry and crumbly with a strong smell and taste. In order for the cheese to turn blue, Italians put a thin copper wire into the cheese, which causes mold to form and the cheese to develop blue veins.

Provolone is another popular cheese. Italians love to use provolone, a salty white cheese, on sandwiches. To acquire its salty taste, provolone cheese is usually aged for several months.

way, and nothing is wasted. When the cheese has been eaten, Italian cooks put the hard, waxy rind that surrounds the cheese into simmering pots of soup. The rind, which is removed before the soup is served, adds a delightful flavor to the dish.

Parmesan cheese is so much a part of Italian cooking that an old Italian saying goes, "Never leave the table if you haven't yet had the taste of Parmesan cheese in your mouth."[4]

Indeed, Italian cooks depend on the delicious taste of Parmesan cheese, tomatoes, garlic, and olive oil to give their cooking its unique and wonderful taste.

Chapter 2

Favorite Foods

Ask any Italian what his or her favorite foods are, and the answer is likely to be pasta, pizza, and **frittatas**. These are the foods Italians adore.

Pasta

Made by mixing flour, water, and salt, pasta may very well be Italy's national dish. Italians eat pasta at least once a day. That means they eat about 60 pounds (27kg) of pasta a year, ten times the amount Americans eat. Usually, Italians eat pasta at the midday meal, which is the largest and most important meal in Italy, just as pasta is Italy's most important food.

Every city and town in Italy has at least one **pastificio** or pasta shop, and many have more. In these shops, fresh

Diners at an outdoor café in Rome enjoy pasta and other delicious foods in view of the Pantheon, a famous ancient temple.

pasta is prepared every day. To entice shoppers, strands of pasta hang appealingly in the window. Inside, hundreds of different kinds of fresh and dried pastas in every shape, size, and color imaginable fill the store. Long pastas, such as linguine; tube pastas, such as macaroni; shaped pastas, such as corkscrew fusilli; and stuffing and layering pastas, such as lasagna, are just a few of the pastas available. These pastas come in a rainbow of colors. Vegetables and spices added to their flour add subtle flavors and bright colors. These additions result in green spinach pasta, red tomato pasta, yellow saffron pasta, purple beet pasta, brown mushroom pasta, and black squid's ink pasta. As Mario Batali says, "There are as many delicious pasta dishes as there are days of the year."[5]

Italians make 300 different varieties of pasta. Italians carefully match each type of pasta to a specific kind of sauce. Long pastas are eaten with smooth sauces, such as tomato or olive oil, which coat the long, thin noodles well. Tubular pastas are paired with chunky vegetable and meat sauces that deliciously fill the noodles' hollows. Shaped pastas work well with sticky cream sauces that cling to them nicely. Italians say that when pastas and sauces are well matched, the result is like poetry.

Chefs prepare several varieties of pasta at a restaurant in the town of Positano. Pasta has been served on Italian tables since Roman times.

Lasagna

Lasagna takes time to make, but it is not difficult. This recipe uses ground beef. Vegetarians can substitute cooked spinach for the beef.

Ingredients:

12 lasagna noodles
1 pound ground beef
1 1/2 jars of spaghetti sauce (about 26 ounces each)
1 container ricotta cheese (about 16 ounces)
2 cups (8 ounces) shredded mozzarella cheese
1/4 cup grated Parmesan cheese
1 egg, beaten
1 teaspoon salt
1/4 teaspoon ground black pepper

Instructions:

1. Heat oven to 350° F.
2. Cook the noodles according to the package directions.
3. While the noodles are cooking, brown the meat in a large skillet.
4. When the meat is brown, remove the skillet from the heat and drain off the excess oil.
5. Stir in the spaghetti sauce and heat until the sauce is hot. Stir frequently.

No matter which sauce is chosen, Italians use only a small amount. That way, the sauce does not overwhelm the taste of the noodles. Pasta, they say, should be lightly coated with sauce rather than smothered with it.

Pasta's Long History

Italians' skill with pasta may be due to the fact that Italians have been eating it for centuries. Archaeologists have unearthed pasta recipes from 1st-century A.D. Rome, and historians say that early Italian explorers

6. Mix the ricotta cheese, egg, salt, pepper, and Parmesan cheese together in a mixing bowl.
7. Spray a 13-inch-by-9-inch baking pan with nonstick cooking spray.
8. Thinly spread a small amount of meat sauce on the bottom of the pan.
9. Put a third of the noodles across the pan.
10. Layer a third of the sauce, a third of the ricotta cheese mixture, and a third of the mozzarella cheese on top of the noodles.
11. Add another row of noodles and repeat the process until all the noodles are used.
12. Top the final row of noodles with sauce and mozzarella cheese.
13. Cover the pan with aluminum foil and place in the oven for about 45 minutes.
14. Then remove the foil and let the lasagna bake for another 10 minutes, or until the sauce is bubbling.
15. Remove from the oven. Allow the lasagna to cool for about 10 minutes and serve.

Serves 6

carried pasta on their ships. Pasta was the perfect food for their long voyages because it could be stored easily without spoiling. Historians think Christopher Columbus probably ate pasta on his trip to the New World. He probably even ate it with a fork, a utensil Italians invented to help them handle the hot, slippery noodles.

Pizza

Like pasta, pizza is another food Italians can't get enough of. Restaurants called pizzerias are everywhere.

Mealtime in Italy

Italians eat three meals a day. La prima colazione, or breakfast, is always a light meal. A typical Italian breakfast consists of a slice of fresh, hot bread and a cup of coffee.

The midday meal is known as il pranzo, or lunch. It usually consists of five courses. The appetizer, or antipasto, is served first. It may consist of a bowl of olives or some fresh cheese. Next, the primo, or first course, is served. The primo is usually soup, pasta, or rice. After the primo, the secondo, or main course, is served. This may be meat, chicken, or seafood. Portions are generally small because Italians have already filled up on the primo. The contorno, or vegetable dish, is served with the secondo. The last course is the dolce, or dessert. Usually it is a bowl of fresh fruit or hard cookies. Wine or mineral water accompanies the meal.

With such a filling lunch, la cena, or supper, is a light meal. Typical suppers include fritatta, pizza, a bowl of soup, or pasta all served with fresh, crusty bread. Supper is eaten around 8:00 P.M.

Italy has 40,000 pizzerias, one for every 1,500 Italians. Compare that to the United States, where there is one pizzeria for every 4,200 people.

Every Italian pizzeria has a large wood-burning oven. Temperatures in these ovens reach 800° F (426° C), so pizzas are cooked in less than two minutes. Italian pizzas are small and irregularly shaped, made to serve one person. Because the crusts are thin and rarely have many toppings, pizza is considered a light meal and is often eaten for supper.

A typical Italian pizza may have two or, at most, three toppings. For instance, tomatoes and garlic top a marinara pizza; mozzarella cheese, olive oil, and spices grace a white pizza; and tomatoes, anchovies, and mozzarella cheese crown a Neapolitan pizza.

The All-Important Crust

The toppings are less important to Italians than the crust. To be good, it must be crispy on the edges and soft in the middle. This type of crust is not easily folded, so Italians eat pizza with a knife and fork.

To make the perfect pizza crust, a cook in a Roman pizzeria tosses kneaded dough high into the air.

A cook in a Naples pizzeria removes a pizza with a golden-brown crust (inset) from a wood-burning oven.

The importance of the crust may be related to the fact that pizza started out as a type of crunchy flat bread, which the ancient Romans topped with herbs, olive oil, and honey. For hundreds of years, pizza was a bread substitute. Only the poorest Italians made it a meal. That changed in 1889, when Italian queen Margherita first tasted pizza. Named "the Margherita" in honor of the queen, that pizza was topped with red tomatoes, white mozzarella cheese, and green basil, just like the red, white, and green of the Italian flag. Queen Margherita loved her namesake, and it soon became a national favorite.

Today pizza is so much a part of Italian life that the World Pizza Making Championship is held in Italy every year. In addition, Italian chefs have developed regulations about pizza making. Pizzerias that meet the regulations proudly display a seal of approval in their windows. In Italy, according to Federico and Stephen Moramarco, "Pizza is a soul food."[6]

The Mezzaluna

When preparing their favorite dishes, Italian cooks often use a mezzaluna. The uniquely shaped knife is an important cutting tool in Italian kitchens.

A mezzaluna is a knife shaped like a half moon. In fact, the word mezzaluna means "half moon" in Italian. The knife has a sharp curved blade that is usually about 10 inches (25cm) in length with two handles.

To use a mezzaluna, the cook firmly holds the handles and rocks the blade back and forth over whatever he or she wants to cut. The mezzaluna makes easy work of chopping hard cheeses, vegetables, meats, and herbs. It can be used to slice or **mince** and is an essential part of every Italian kitchen.

The dual-handled knife known as a mezzaluna is an important cutting tool in Italian kitchens.

Frittatas

Another food Italians love is the frittata. A frittata is an open-faced Italian omelet. It is a delicious dish that Italians enjoy eating for a light supper or as an **appetizer** during the midday meal. The only time Italians do not eat frittatas is for breakfast. That's the time for coffee and bread.

Like omelets, frittatas are made with any number of ingredients. They are fun to make as well as economical. Most Italians make frittatas with whatever ingredients they have on hand. Frittata fillings are likely to change with the season and the cook's mood. And leftovers often find their way into the tastiest frittatas.

A frittata may contain cheese, potatoes, mushrooms, peppers, tomatoes, zucchini, asparagus, peas, garlic, pasta covered with sauce, ham, bacon, or sausage, in any number of combinations. But no matter what other ingredients are used, most frittatas contains eggs, onions, and olive oil. Many are made with these three ingredients alone. That may be why Italian peasants were the first to make the dish. Even in the worst of times, eggs, onions, and olive oil were available to rural people. But once city dwellers tasted frittatas, the omelets became popular throughout Italy.

Frittatas are easy to make. Unlike American omelets, frittatas are not folded or flipped. Instead, the eggs and

Cheese Frittata

This is a simple and tasty frittata. To add onions and other vegetables, chop them and brown them in the olive oil before adding the eggs.

Ingredients:

2 tablespoons olive oil
8 eggs
salt and pepper to taste
$3/4$ cup shredded mozzarella or provolone
 cheese

Instructions:

1. Heat the oil over medium heat in a large oven-safe skillet.
2. Crack the eggs into a large bowl. Beat the eggs and add salt and pepper to taste.
3. When the eggs are well beaten, pour them into the skillet.
4. Cook the eggs for 3 to 5 minutes.
5. When the bottom of the eggs is set, sprinkle the cheese on top of the eggs.
6. Put the skillet with the eggs and cheese in the broiler for about 3 minutes, or until the eggs are puffed and the cheese is golden and bubbly.
7. Cut into wedges. Serve hot or cold with Italian bread.

Serves 4

other ingredients are cooked in a skillet until the eggs are almost done. Then the skillet is put in a broiler for just a few minutes. This turns the top of the frittata golden brown. The finished frittata is often brought to the table in the hot skillet, where it is cut into pie-shaped wedges and served hot. The frittata also may be cooled, sliced, and carried by workers and schoolchildren in their lunch boxes or taken on family picnics. Every Italian grows up eating this simple, tasty dish. Nick Stellino, an Italian-born chef, recalls, "Springtime in Sicily. . . . The Stellinos and their friends are already on the lookout for an outdoor dining adventure. For our most satisfying picnics, frittatas were always on the menu."[7]

It is not only in Sicily where frittatas rule. Travelers can go from Milan in northern Italy to the far south, and they will find Italians eating frittatas, pizza, and pasta everywhere along the way. Ingredients may vary, but the taste is always delicious. It is no wonder why Italians love these foods.

Snacks and Sweets

When Italians want a treat, they have many delicious snacks and sweets to choose from. Italy is known for its delicious ice creams, ices, and cookies. Italians are also fond of **paninis**, bite-sized sandwiches perfect for snacking.

Panini: A Healthy Snack

A panini is the equivalent of Italian fast food. But unlike most American fast food, a panini is not fried or loaded with artificial ingredients. Instead, it is a fresh and healthy snack.

Morning, afternoon, and night, cafés and bars all over Italy sell these little sandwiches to hungry Italians on the go. And street vendors sell hot paninis to Italian

An array of mouthwatering paninis on display at a food stand on Venice's Rialto Bridge tempts passersby.

schoolchildren who flock to panini stands set up around Italian schools.

A Grilled Sandwich

Like most sandwiches, a panini is made by filling a small roll, or two slices of crusty bread, with any number of combinations of vegetables, meats, and cheeses. Sometimes a panini is eaten cold. But most often, the sandwich is placed in a cast-iron press, known as a panini press, and is put over a hot grill to toast. The press flattens the sandwich,

A country woman in Tuscany walks with loaves of freshly baked bread. Paninis can be made with many different kinds of bread.

Cheese, Ham, and Tomato Panini

This is a typical panini. The filling can be changed to suit the cook's taste and imagination. Turkey, salami, or chicken can be used in place of the ham. Any favorite cheese also can be used. Sliced Italian bread can be used in place of the rolls.

Ingredients:

4 hard rolls, sliced in half
4 slices mozzarella or provolone cheese
4 slices ham
8 slices tomato, large
2 tablespoons olive oil
mustard to taste

Instructions:

1. Lightly spread the mustard on the bottom half of the rolls.
2. Layer a slice of cheese, a slice of ham, and two slices of tomato on top.
3. Close the sandwiches with the top halves of the rolls.
4. Brush olive oil over both sides of the sandwiches.
5. Cook sandwiches on a grill over medium heat or in a broiler for 3 minutes per side, until the bread is toasted and the cheese is melted. Serve hot.

Serves 4

allowing the flavors to deliciously blend together. The result is a hot, flavorful treat.

A typical panini might contain tomato, mozzarella cheese, and salami. Italians only use a few fillings in a panini. This is because they do not want the different flavors to overpower each other. In the perfect panini, the bread and filling complement each other. Italians have been perfecting this balance for hundreds of years. They were snacking on paninis long before the Earl of Sandwich introduced the sandwich in England in the 18th century.

A Perfect Match

A panini can be made with dozens of different types of breads and hundreds of fillings. Italians carefully match panini fillings and bread. Not everyone agrees on what goes best together. Italians, a cook explains, "discuss at length and even fight over which breads are best with which stuffing."[8] When the discussion is over, there is one thing every Italian can agree on: Italians love paninis!

Granitas and Gelato

When Italians want a sweet snack, they head for a gelateria, an Italian café that sells **granitas** (Italian ices) and **gelato** (Italian ice cream).

Granitas are similar to American snow cones. But granitas are made by hand rather than in a machine. A granita is a frozen mix of water, sugar, and a flavorful base such as watermelon, lemon, orange, or **espresso**, a strong Italian coffee. Because granitas contain four times more flavoring than sugar, the flavor is intense and not as sweet as the ices Americans usually eat.

A Summer Treat

Italians say that nothing is as refreshing as a granita. And they should know—they've been eating granitas for thousands of years. Ancient **Sicilians** routinely poured orange-flavored syrup over snow they gathered

Italian Pastries

When Italians want a sweet dessert, they have a number of delicious pastries to choose from. One of Italy's most popular pastries is tiramisu, a light coffee-flavored cake. To make tiramisu, pieces of spongy yellow cake that are shaped like a woman's finger are soaked in coffee and are layered with mascarpone cheese, a sweet Italian cheese. They are then dusted with cocoa powder.

A cannoli is another delicious Italian pastry. A cannoli consists of a horn-shaped pastry shell that is fried to make it crisp and delectable. Sometimes the shell is dipped in chocolate. The shell is then filled with thick, sweet cream made from ricotta cheese, sugar, spices, and cocoa.

A cassata is an Italian cake. Also known as cannoli cake, a cassata is a yellow sponge cake layered with cannoli cream and decorated with sliced almonds. Sometimes cassatas are made with chocolate cake. Either way, cassatas are a tasty treat.

A gelato truck on a street in Rome sells gelato and granitas, the delicious frozen treats that are a favorite summertime snack.

in the winter from Mt. Etna. Today, Italians do not have to wait for winter to enjoy granitas. In fact, granitas are a favorite summer snack. In the hot summer, Italians eat granitas from early morning until late at night. Many Italians substitute espresso-flavored granita for their breakfast coffee. And beachgoers flock to grattachecches, or granita vendors, who walk the sandy beaches selling the icy treat. As Barry Lazar, a cook and

Huge stacks of sugar cones in a Florence gelateria entice customers to try a scoop or two of their favorite gelato.

an Italian traveler, says, "They are Italy's gift to a summer day."[9]

Granitas with Milk

Gelato, the name given to Italian ice cream, is a granita in which milk has been substituted for water. Historians believe Italians invented gelato in 1565. At that time, Bernardo Buontalenti, an Italian architect, chilled sweet cream in a special room he had designed to keep

Orange Granita

Granitas are simple to make. All you need is water, sugar, fruit juice, and a freezer. This is a recipe for an orange granita. By switching the flavoring, it can become any flavor granita the cook wants. Lemon juice, pineapple juice, grapefruit juice, or coffee can be easily substituted for the orange juice to make lemon, pineapple, grapefruit, or coffee granitas.

Ingredients:

3 cups water
1/3 cup sugar to taste
1 cup orange juice

Instructions:

1. In a mixing bowl, stir 1 cup of water with the sugar. Stir until all the sugar is dissolved.
2. Add the orange juice and remaining water.
3. Stir well. The mixture will be syrupy.
4. Transfer the mixture to a metal pie dish or a flat pan. Place it in the freezer.
5. Stir every 30 minutes. The granita is done when it is slightly slushy.

Serves 6.

ice. The frozen treat was served to the royal Medici family, who loved it. Thus, ice cream was born.

In many ways gelato is similar to American ice cream, but gelato contains less air, which makes it thicker and richer. And, like granitas, gelato's flavor is intense because it contains more flavoring than sugar.

Fruit Flavors

Italians eat gelato in cones or cups. Unlike Americans, who eat one scoop per flavor, Italians mix a variety of flavors in one scoop.

And, what flavors there are! Fruit flavors are favorites and include almost every fruit known—grapefruits, figs, tangerines, plums, pears, melons, apricots, peaches, and apples are just a few. Chocolate gelato may be bittersweet or white, and coffee gelatos taste surprisingly like a creamy frozen version of the beverage. Walnut, hazelnut, almond, and chestnut gelatos are sweet and crunchy.

A Serious Food

Italians take gelato very seriously. By law, gelaterias must post the ingredients of their gelatos where customers can easily see them. This allows Italians to be sure they are getting the best quality gelato their money can buy. On a typical summer day, gelaterias are crowded with Italians savoring gelatos. Viana La Place, an American who spends her summers in Italy, explains: "During my summers in Italy, I, along with every single Italian, young and old, live on . . . gelato. It is simply one of the rituals involved with eating and living and being Italian."[10]

Biscottis

Another favorite Italian snack and popular dessert is a hard cookie known as a **biscotti.** Biscottis are long, dry, crisp cookies that are baked

Italians enjoy Gelato at an outdoor café in Verona.

Espresso

Another favorite Italian treat is espresso, a strong black coffee. Unlike American coffee, which is made when hot water gently drips on ground coffee, espresso is made in a special espresso machine. The machine forces hot water under pressure through ground coffee. This makes the brewed coffee quite strong. Because of its strength, espresso is served in tiny 3-ounce (.09 liters) cups. Most Italians do not drink espresso first thing in the morning. Instead, they stop at a coffee bar on their way to work. Each morning, crowds of Italians stand at coffee-bar counters, where they sip the powerful drink.

twice to give them a unique, crunchy flavor. Biscottis are not very sweet, but because of their texture they are perfect for dunking. Italians love to dunk biscottis into their coffee during the day and into their leftover wine after supper. In fact, when an Italian child is allowed to dunk a biscotti into some wine, it is a sign that he or she is growing up. And, when Italians are not dunking biscottis, they are likely to top the cookies with fruit, melted chocolate, a handful of nuts, or gelato.

Many Flavors

Biscottis come in many flavors. Traditional biscottis are flavored with almonds and anise, a licorice-flavored herb. The first biscottis were almond flavored and were created by a 15th-century Italian baker who wanted a crisp cookie to serve with wine. They became wildly popular. Italians loved their crisp texture and the fact that the cookies could be stored for months without spoiling. Their long shelf life made them a staple in every Italian kitchen as well as on the ships of Italian explorers.

Over time, different flavorings were tried. Today, biscottis are made with almost every nut, fruit, chocolate, and spice. Combinations such as chocolate-hazelnut,

A woman rolls dough to make biscotti, while her friend prepares ingredients for another Italian dish.

espresso-orange, and honey-walnut are just a few of the many types of biscottis Italians love.

Twice Baked

Despite the flavoring, all biscottis are made in the same way. First, the dough is shaped into a log and is then baked until it is firm. It is then cut into long $1/2$-thick (1.27cm-thick) cookies that are baked again. The second baking removes moisture from the dough. This gives biscottis their dry, crunchy texture.

Every Italian eats biscottis. They are a snack, a dessert, and even a common breakfast food. Bakeries all over Italy make their own special biscottis, which they sell in large family-size bags. A baker explains that, in Italy, biscottis are "associated with simple pleasures and joyous occasions."[11]

Between paninis, granitas, gelato, and biscottis, the lives of Italians are filled with many pleasures. These delicious snacks and sweets add flavor and fun to every Italian's life.

Foods for Holidays and Celebrations

Italians love to eat. Holidays give them a chance to celebrate with friends and family while enjoying special holiday foods.

The Feast of the Seven Fish

Christmas Eve and seafood go together. Most Italians give up meat on the day before Christmas for religious reasons. But that doesn't mean Italians give up celebrating. Even without meat, Italians manage to make Christmas Eve supper a feast. The meal consists of seven different fish dishes, one for each day of the week. Maryann Nichole Ruperto, whose family is Italian, says, "In my family Christmas Eve has always been our favorite day of the year. Not just because of the

An Italian woman serves up heaping plates of pasta as her family sits down to enjoy a meal together.

wonderful holiday but because it is our favorite meal of the year, our fish dinner."[12]

Squid, octopus, clams, eel, lobster, crab, shrimp, flounder, codfish, salmon, and tuna fish are just a few of the delicacies that crowd Italian tables. They may be fried, grilled, baked, served cold in cocktails, boiled into thick chowders, stuffed in pasta, tossed in salads, drizzled with olive oil and spices, or covered by rich sauces. Squid, or **calamari**, as it is called in Italy, is usually stuffed with garlic and cheese, covered with tomato sauce, and served tentacles and all. **Capitone**, which are big, fat eels, are traditionally dredged

A worker unloads crates of fish at a market in the town of Mondello. Seafood is a major part of the Italian diet.

Fish heads, an important ingredient in Italian stews, sit alongside other cuts of fish for sale at a market in Naples.

in flour and fried. Because eels shed their skin only to replace it with new skin, to Italians, eating eel on Christmas Eve symbolizes renewal and new beginnings in the coming year.

Baccala

No matter what other fish dishes make it to the holiday table, **baccala** is always served. Made of codfish that is dried outdoors in the wind and then preserved under salt, baccala is not easy to prepare. It takes at least two days to ready the fish for the table. Dried baccala is thin, salty, and hard. To remove the salt and soften it,

Italian Seafood Salad

Cold seafood salad is frequently one of the seven fish dishes served on Christmas Eve. This recipe calls for cooked, peeled, and deveined shrimp, which can be purchased in most supermarkets.

Ingredients:

3 cups (8 ounces) shell or bow-tie pasta
$1/2$-pound cooked fresh shrimp, peeled and deveined
2 celery stalks, chopped
1 sweet red pepper, chopped
1 sweet yellow pepper, chopped
$1/4$ cup chopped red onion
$1/2$ cup sliced, pitted black olives
$1/4$ cup olive oil
5 tablespoons fresh lemon juice
2 cloves garlic, minced
salt and ground black pepper to taste
1 ounce anchovy fillets, drained and chopped (optional)

Instructions:

1. Cook the pasta according to the package directions.
2. Drain the pasta and place in a large bowl.
3. Add the shrimp, peppers, onions, olives, and celery. Toss together.
4. In another bowl, stir together the olive oil, lemon juice, garlic, salt, and pepper.
5. Pour the oil mixture over the pasta mixture and toss.
6. Cover the salad and refrigerate for at least one hour.
7. Top with anchovies before serving (optional).
8. Serve the salad cold.

Serves 4 to 6

Chocolate Eggs

Chocolate eggs are a popular Easter treat. Brightly wrapped chocolate Easter eggs, or uovis di Pasqua, are sold in pastry shops throughout Italy. They can be as small as 1/3 ounce (9g) or as large as 18 pounds (8kg). The smaller eggs are for children, and the larger ones are for adults. No matter their size, the eggs contain a surprise inside. This may be a tiny toy for a child or a small picture frame for an adult. Some eggs are custom made and contain fabulous gifts such as a set of new car keys or a diamond ring.

cooks beat the fish with a little wooden mallet. They then soak it in multiple changes of water, squeezing out excess liquid and salt after each soaking. This is done by sandwiching the wet fish between two cutting boards topped by a weight, such as a stack of books.

Once the fish resumes its fresh-caught shape and texture, it is dredged in flour and slowly cooked in milk with olive oil, garlic, and Parmesan cheese. Because baccala is cooked until all the milk is absorbed and the fish is soft enough to cut with a spoon, the cooking process takes about three hours. But it is not done yet! Finally, the baccala is refrigerated for 24 hours before it is served cold on Christmas Eve.

Viking Cod

Italians have perfected this complicated ritual over hundreds of years. Dried cod was first brought to Italy in 1432, after Piero Querini, an Italian explorer, had been shipwrecked near Norway. His Viking rescuers introduced him to the salty fish. He brought it back to Italy, where it became popular. Italians loved its taste and the fact that, unlike fresh fish, it did not spoil. It was not long before they created their own way of preparing it.

Today, because baccala takes so long to prepare, many modern Italians use fresh cod instead of the dried, salted kind. No matter how the fish is prepared, Christmas Eve in Italy would not be the same without it. As one Italian explains, "While tradition allows for some flexibility in the seven fish menu, there is one item that is totally non-negotiable. Baccala must absolutely show on the Christmas Eve table."[13]

Panettone on Christmas Day

The feasting does not end on Christmas Eve. Italians enjoy another banquet on Christmas day. In fact, many cooks start preparing the meal days in advance. Salads, pastas, soups, beef, lamb, ham, and vegetables all weigh down the Christmas table. But no matter how much Italians eat, they always leave room for **panettone**, Italy's favorite Christmas dessert.

Light and spongy, panettone is a delicious cake made with lots of eggs, butter, candied fruit, and raisins. Its unique shape—tall with a wide, round top—resembles the many domed churches and cathedrals throughout Italy. That may be why it is so popular at Christmas, when Italians purchase about 68 million panettones. Since Italy's total population is about 57 million, that's more than one cake per person. Sold in tall, brightly colored boxes, panettone is a wildly popular Christmas gift. Deborah Mele, an Italian writer, recalls, "It wasn't unusual for our family to have almost a dozen panettone in our cupboard when the season was over."[14]

Happily Ever After

There are many stories about the origins of panettone. According to one popular tale, a 15th-century Italian fell in love with the daughter of a baker named Toni. In an effort to impress the girl's father and win her hand in marriage, the man created the oddly shaped cake and named it Pan di Toni, or "Toni's bread," after his beloved's father. The sweet treat was an immediate success with the baker and all of his customers. So, of course, the couple was allowed to marry and lived happily ever after.

Over the years, panettone has become associated with Christmas. Served with espresso or wine, it may be topped with chocolate sauce or gelato, or eaten plain. Traditionally,

A large group of locals enjoys an outdoor fest during an annual summer festival in the town of Sienna.

each family member takes a bite of the first three slices of the cake. By doing so, Italians believe they will ensure good luck until next Christmas.

Easter Pie

Easter gives Italians another chance to eat heartily. Because most Italians give up their favorite foods during Lent, a 40-day period before Easter, Easter Sunday is a time for Italians to make up for their sacrifices and enjoy the richest dishes imaginable. That may be why Easter dinner is a big, multicourse meal that usually begins with a slice of Easter pie, a rich and satisfying treat.

A woman in Pizzo balances cartons of eggs, the key ingredient in Easter pie, on her head.

Not a sweet pastry, Easter pie, or torta di Pasqua, consists of layer upon layer of different meats, cheeses, and eggs encased in a buttery crust. "What better way to bid farewell to the season of fasting and penitence than with a dish that offers three kinds of ham and up to six kinds of cheese, plus eggs and butter?"[15] Domenica Marchetti, an Italian food writer, comments.

A typical pie contains six different types of cheeses. Soft and semi-soft cheeses, such as ricotta and mozzarella, which melt and bake easily, are among the most popular. Pork is the most common meat used. Layers of sausage, ham, bacon, and pepperoni blend deliciously. But no matter what else is added to the recipe, Easter pie always has plenty of eggs, usually about a dozen. They may be hard boiled, sliced, and layered beneath the meat and

Easter Pie

Any prepared pie crust can be used in this recipe. The recipe calls for prosciutto, a type of Italian ham with a salty flavor. If prosciutto is unavailable, any other type of ham or cooked sausage can be used in its place. Cottage cheese may be substituted for ricotta cheese.

Ingredients:

1 pie crust—top and bottom
1 pound ricotta cheese
5 hard-boiled eggs, sliced
5 eggs
$1/4$ pound salami, chopped
$1/4$ pound mozzarella cheese, shredded
$1/4$ pound prosciutto, or other ham, chopped
salt and pepper to taste

Instructions:

1. Preheat the oven to 350° F.
2. In a bowl, mix together the ricotta cheese, hard-boiled eggs, salami, mozzarella cheese, and prosciutto.
3. In another bowl, beat together the raw eggs.
4. Add the beaten eggs to the cheese, meat, and hard-boiled egg mixture. Mix well.
5. Put the meat mixture into the bottom pie crust.
6. Cover with the top crust. Crimp the edges to seal the pie closed. Cut 4 slits in the top of the pie crust.
7. Bake for 1 hour or until the crust is golden brown. Let the pie cool for about 30 minutes. Slice and serve.

Serves 8

Lucky Lentils

Italians always eat lentils on New Year's Day. Because they look like tiny coins, lentils represent wealth to Italians. Italians say that the more lentils a person eats on New Year's Day, the more money he or she will earn in the new year.

cheese, or the eggs may be beaten and allowed to bake in the pie, forming a custardlike filling. Often cooked and uncooked eggs both find their way under the crust. This is because, to Italians, eggs, which are associated with re-birth, symbolize Easter.

No one knows when Easter pies originated. One story says that the first Easter pie was made with grain that ar-rived in Italy on a foreign ship during a time of famine. Be-cause the ship was unexpected, its arrival was considered a miracle, just as, to Christians, the events that occurred on the first Easter are also considered miraculous. Over time, the layered pie became synonymous with Easter for Italians.

Easter pie, panettone, the seven fish dishes, and bac-cala are just a few of the many traditional dishes that add delicious flavor to Italian holidays. Italians know that the combination of good food, good friends, and family make every Italian celebration memorable.

Metric Conversions

Mass (weight)

1 ounce (oz.) = 28.0 grams (g)
8 ounces = 227.0 grams
1 pound (lb.)
  or 16 ounces = 0.45 kilograms (kg)
2.2 pounds = 1.0 kilogram

Liquid Volume

1 teaspoon (tsp.) = 5.0 milliliters (ml)
1 tablespoon (tbsp.) = 15.0 milliliters
1 fluid ounce (oz.) = 30.0 milliliters
1 cup (c.) = 240 milliliters
1 pint (pt.) = 480 milliliters
1 quart (qt.) = 0.95 liters (l)
1 gallon (gal.) = 3.80 liters

Pan Sizes

8-inch cake pan = 20 x 4-centimeter cake pan
9-inch cake pan = 23 x 3.5-centimeter cake pan
11 x 7-inch baking pan = 28 x 18-centimeter baking pan
13 x 9-inch baking pan = 32.5 x 23-centimeter baking pan
9 x 5-inch loaf pan = 23 x 13-centimeter loaf pan
2-quart casserole = 2-liter casserole

Temperature

212° F = 100° C (boiling point of water)
225° F = 110° C
250° F = 120° C
275° F = 135° C
300° F = 150° C
325° F = 160° C
350° F = 180° C
375° F = 190° C
400° F = 200° C

Length

1/4 inch (in.) = 0.6 centimeters (cm)
1/2 inch = 1.25 centimeters
1 inch = 2.5 centimeters

55

Chapter 1: The Heart and Soul of Italian Cooking

1. Mario Batali, *Simple Italian Food.* New York: Clarkson Potter, 1998, p. 57.
2. Quoted in Franchi Sementi, "Seeds of Italy." www.seedsofitaly.sagenet.co.uk.
3. Quoted in La Belle Cuisine, "La Belle Cuisine—More Essentials." www.labellecuisine.com/Basics/Roasted%20Garlic.htm.
4. Quoted in Carol Field, *In Nonna's Kitchen.* New York: HarperCollins, 1997, p. 34.

Chapter 2: Favorite Foods

5. Batali, *Simple Italian Food,* p. 76.
6. Federico Moramarco and Stephen Moramarco, "101 Reasons to Be Proud You're Italian," Rome Gift Shop.com. http://store.yahoo.com/romegiftshop/101reastobep.html.
7. Nick Stellino, *Cucina Amore.* New York: Doubleday, 1995, p. 93.

Chapter 3: Snacks and Sweets

8. Il Forno, "Between Two Slices." www.ilforno.typepad.com/il_forno/between_two_slices.

9. Barry Lazar, "Gelato and Granita," Montreal Foods. www.montrealfood.com/granita.html.

10. Viana La Place, *La Bella Cucina.* New York: Clarkson Potter, 2001, p. 204.

11. Award Baking, "A Taste of History." www.award baking.com/history.html.

Chapter 4: Foods for Holidays and Celebrations

12. Maryann Nichole Ruperto, "The Tale of the Fishes." www.neuronet.pitt.edu/~mruperto/fishes.htm.

13. Patrice D. Bucciarelli, "Pour the Wine, Pass the Baccala: Traditional Italian Holiday Foods," Accenti Online. www.accenti.ca/article_cover.php.

14. Deborah Mele, "An Italian Christmas," Italian Food Forever. www.italianfoodforever.com/iff/articles.asp?id=37.

15. Domenica Marchetti, "A Slice of Italian Tradition," Sicilian Culture, March 27, 2002. www.sicilianculture.com/news/2002-pizzarustica.htm.

Glossary

appetizer: A light food served before a meal.

baccala: Dried and salted codfish.

biscotti: A long, crisp Italian cookie.

calamari: The Italian word for squid, a popular seafood in Italy.

capitone: The Italian name for fried eel.

cuisine: The food of a particular group or nation.

espresso: Strong Italian coffee.

frittatas: Italian omelets.

garlic braids: Garlic cloves that are woven together to form long braids.

gelato: Italian ice cream.

granitas: Italian ices.

mince: To chop into very small pieces.

panettone: An Italian cake served at Christmas.

paninis: Italian sandwiches.

pasta: The Italian word for noodles.

pastificio: A store in which pasta is made and sold.

pizza: The Italian word for pie.

Sicilians: People who live on the southern Italian island of Sicily.

for further Exploration

Books

Alison Behnke, *Italy in Pictures*. Minneapolis: Lerner, 2002. Life in Italy is discussed and depicted in pictures.

Deanna F. Cook, *The Kids Multicultural Cookbook: Food and Fun Around the World*. Charlotte, VT: Williamson, 1995. Recipes and fun facts from around the world, including Italy.

Sylvia Johnson, *Tomatoes, Potatoes, Corn, and Beans*. New York: Atheneum Books for Young Readers, 1997. This book talks about the origins of tomatoes, among other foods, and explains how the Italians adopted the fruit as their own.

Pamela Marx, *Travel the World Cookbook*. Tuscon, AZ: Good Year, 1996. Recipes, food facts, and craft activities from around the world, including Italy.

Christine Peterson and David Peterson, *Italy*. Danbury, CT: Childrens Press, 2002. This book talks about the geography, history, and daily life in Italy with maps and pictures.

Kristen Thoennes, *Christmas in Italy*. Manakato, MN: Capstone, 1999. This book discusses how Christmas is celebrated in Italy, with a look at the foods served.

Web Sites

Italian Food Forever (www.italianfoodforever.com). This Web site offers dozens of different recipes with photos.

Think Quest (thinkquest.org/library/cat_show.html?cat_id=85). Among its many categories, this Web site for children has a section on pizza, cultures, countries and cuisines, and food history.

Virtual Italia (virtualitalia.com). Take a virtual trip to Italy with pictures, stories, and recipes.

Index

Picture Credits

About the Author

Barbara Sheen has been an author and educator for more than thirty years. She writes in English and Spanish. Her writing has been published in the United States and Europe. She lives in New Mexico with her family. In her spare time, she likes to swim, bike, garden, read, and cook. She loves Italian food!